A Little Book
of Francis
# of Assisi

Compiled and introduced by
Don Mullan

BOOKS & MEDIA

ISBN 0-8198-4497-7

Published in the USA by
Pauline Books & Media,
50 Saint Paul's Avenue,
Boston, MA 02130-3491.
www.pauline.org

Pauline Books & Media is the publishing house of the Daughters of St Paul, an international congregation of women religious serving the Church with the communications media.

1 2 3 4 5 6 7 8 9   10 09 08 07 06 05 04 03 02

To
Fr Gerry Raftery OFM
and
to the memory of
Dom Helder Camara

Acknowledgements

The publisher and editor gratefully acknowledge the permission of the following to quote from material in their copyright: Paulist Press for quotations from *Francis and Clare – The Complete Works*, translated and introduced by Regis J. Armstrong OFM Cap and Ignatius C. Brady OFM; SPCK for quotations from *St Francis of Assisi – Omnibus of Sources (1973)*, edited by Marion A. Habig.

Author's Acknowledgements

Sincere thanks are owed to the following for their kind support and assistance with this publication:

Fr Ulic Troy OFM, Minister Provincial, Franciscan Province of Ireland and the Franciscan Provincial Definitory; Fr Gerry Raftery OFM for his friendship and guidance; Bernie Bergin for her assistance with parallel reading and much goodwill, good humour and encouragement; Seamus Cashman; John Scally and Emer Ryan for their continued friendship; the following members of the Franciscan Family for their varied and most helpful suggestions (my apologies in advance for not being able to incorporate all): Sr M. Patrick

MacCarthy; Sr M. Louis O'Donovan; Sr M. Faustina; Sr M. Paul; Sr Agnes Horgan; Sr M. Anthony; Sr Thérèse Marie Crowe; Sr Mary Gabriel Francis; Sr M. Catherine; Sr Mary; Sr M. Brigid; Fr Richard Callanan OFM; Sr Catherine O'Bierne and Franciscan Missionaries of Mary; Sr Joseph FSM; Sr Bridget Veale; Sr Johanna Kelly FMSJ; Catherine Finnegan; Sr Nora Davis FMM; Sr Kathleen Lynch FMDM; Fr Lorcán Mac Aodhán; The Franciscans/ Na Proinsiasaigh; and Fr Owen O'Sullivan OFM Cap for his generous sharing of personal quotes. Finally, to my family, Margaret, Thérèse, Carl and Emma for their continued kindness and support.

INTRODUCTION

St Francis of Assisi was born in 1182. As a youth he entertained illusions of grandeur and aspired to be a knight in shining armour. At the age of 23, however, he experienced a conversion of heart. While visiting the tumbledown ruins of St Damiano Church on the outskirts of Assisi he heard a voice that said, 'Repair my Church'. Francis responded literally to the command but later realised it had much wider implications for the spiritual rebuilding of the universal Christian church, then in need of urgent renewal and reawakening.

The essence of Francis of Assisi is his joyful simplicity and unconditional surrender to the poverty of the gospels. His writings are often a remarkable interlinking of diverse sentences that reveal a profound grasp of scriptural texts.

Almost eight centuries after his death in 1226, Francis of Assisi continues to fascinate and inspire people of all faiths, and none, throughout the globe. Hundreds of thousands of men and women follow Francis today in a variety of religious and secular orders.

His union with God was such that he held within his being a real, yet mystical, fusion of all creation that he revered with the intimacy of an affectionate sibling. All creation, from the immensity of the cosmos to the smallest insect, spoke to him of God. Primarily, however, it was in loving his neighbour, in a spirit of respect, gentleness, courtesy, generosity and unselfishness, that Francis of Assisi was a reflection of his master, Jesus. A weaver of harmony, he offers an inspiring example of peacemaking to a deeply troubled world.

At a critical moment in the history of humanity and Christianity, the teachings and reflections of St Francis retain an urgency that is as relevant today as it was at the time of his hearing the command, 'Repair my Church'. The following quotations and prayers are the living words of a universal saint whose message is needed now – more than ever before!

Don Mullan
Dublin
22 August 2002

PEACE

Since you speak of peace,
all the more so
must you have it in your hearts.

PEACE

The hand must *not* be quickly laid
to the sword.

PEACE

Let none be provoked to anger
or scandal by you,
but rather may they be drawn to peace,
goodwill and concord
through your gentleness.

PEACE

We have been called to heal wounds,
to unite what has fallen apart,
and to bring home those
who have lost their way.
Many who may seem to us to be
children of the devil
will still become Christ's disciples.

Service of God

Let us begin to serve the Lord God,
for up to now
we have made little or no progress.

SERVICE OF GOD

It is sweet to the body to commit sin
and it is bitter for it to serve God.

SERVICE OF GOD

The truly pure of heart are those who despise the things of earth and seek the things of heaven, and who never cease to adore and behold the Lord God loving and true with a pure heart and soul.

SERVICE OF GOD

Live always in truth
That you may die in obedience.

Do not look at the life outside,
For that of the Spirit is better.

SERVICE OF GOD

I beg you through great love,
To use with discretion
The alms which the Lord gives you.

SERVICE OF GOD

Most high, glorious God,
enlighten the darkness of my heart
and give me, Lord,
a correct faith,
a certain hope,
a perfect charity,
sense and knowledge,
so that I may carry out
your holy and true command.

SERVICE OF GOD

Believe me, the Mother of God
would rather have
the gospel of her son observed
and her altar stripped
than have the altar adorned
and her son scorned.

LOVE

Love softens all things
and makes every bitter thing sweet.

LOVE

Blessed is the servant
who would love his brother
as much when he is sick
and cannot repay him
as he would when he is well
and can repay him.

LOVE

Let us love our neighbours as ourselves.
And if there is anyone
who does not wish to love them as himself,
at least let him do no harm to them,
but rather good.

LOVE

Express love for one another by deeds,
as the apostle says:
Let us not love in word or speech,
but in deed and in truth.
And slander no one.

LOVE

Courtesy is one of the qualities of God,
who courteously gives his sun
and his rain and everything
to the just and to the unjust.
And courtesy is a sister of charity.
It extinguishes hatred and keeps love alive.

LOVE

Blessed is that friar who loves
and respects his brother
as much when he is absent
as when he is present
and who would not say anything
behind his back
that he could not say charitably to his face.

SIN

No one is to be obliged to obey another
in anything by which a sin
or a crime is committed.

SIN

It seems to me that I am
the greatest of sinners,
for if God had treated any criminal
with such great mercy,
he would have been
ten times more spiritual than I.

The Sick

I beg all my sick brothers that they do not
become angry in their infirmities or
disturbed either against God
or against their brothers ...
Let them give thanks in all things,
so that they may desire to be
as God wants them to be.

THE SICK

Lord, help me in my infirmities
so that I may have the strength
to bear them patiently.

THE SICK

When I was in sin,
it seemed extremely bitter to me
to look at lepers,
and the Lord himself led me among them
and I practised mercy with them.

FAITH

Cast your thought upon the Lord,
and he will nourish you.

FAITH

Go and do not worry …
Do not say that something is impossible.

FAITH

If the body takes its food in quiet
which, along with itself,
will become the food of worms,
with what great peace and tranquillity
should not the soul take its food,
which is God himself.

FAITH

The Blessed Christ
never hardens the heart
of the faithful one
but rather softens it,
as he says through the Prophet:
'I will take away your heart of stone
and will give you a heart of flesh.'

GOD'S LOVE FOR US

Let no temptation disturb you;
let no thought exasperate you;
for you are very dear to me.

GOD'S LOVE FOR US

Let the whole of humankind tremble ...
that the Lord of the universe,
God and the Son of God,
so humbles himself
that for our salvation
he hides himself
under the little form of bread.

GOD'S LOVE FOR US

Greatly to be loved is his love,
who loved us so greatly.

GOD'S LOVE FOR US

May the power of your love, O Lord,
fiery and sweet as honey,
wean my heart from all that is under heaven
so that I may die for love of your love,
you who were so good
as to die for love of my love.

CREATURES

My brothers, birds,
you should praise your Creator very much
and always love him;
he gave you feathers to clothe you,
wings so that you can fly,
and whatever else was necessary for you.
God made you noble among his creatures
and he gave you a home
in the purity of the air.

CREATURES

My sisters, swallows,
it is now time for me to speak,
for you have already spoken enough.
Listen to the word of the Lord
and be silent and quiet
until the word of the Lord is finished.

CREATURES

Be conscious, O human,
of the wondrous state
in which the Lord God has placed you …
all the creatures under heaven,
each according to its nature,
serve, know, and obey their Creator
better than you.

THE POOR

A certain man asked
to be admitted into the order.
'If you wish to be joined with the poor,
first distribute your possessions
to the poor of the world.'
The man left and distributed his goods
to his relatives
and gave nothing to the poor.

THE POOR

When he came back
the saint laughed and said:
'Go on your way,
for you have defrauded the poor;
you have laid an unsound foundation
on which to build a spiritual structure.'

THE POOR

Who curses a poor man
does an injury to Christ,
whose noble image he wears,
the image of him
who made himself poor
for us in this world.

THE POOR

Let us have charity and humility;
let us give alms
since this washes from our souls
the stain of sin.

THE POOR

Rejoice when among people who are looked down upon, among the poor and the powerless, the sick and the lepers, and the beggars by the wayside. You should not be ashamed, but rather recall that our Lord Jesus Christ, the Son of the living and all-powerful God … was a poor man and a transient and lived on alms.

THE POOR

Everything that people leave behind
in the world will perish,
but for the charity and the almsgiving
which they have done
they will receive a reward from the Lord.

POOR IN SPIRIT

You are all our riches.

Poverty is the special way to salvation;
its fruit is manifold,
but it is really well known only to a few.

POOR IN SPIRIT

Those who came to receive life
gave to the poor everything which they
were capable of possessing and they were
content with one tunic, patched inside and
out, with a cord and short trousers. And
we had no desire for anything more.

POOR IN SPIRIT

If we had any possessions we should also
be forced to have arms to protect them,
since possessions are a cause of disputes
and strife, and in many ways we should be
hindered from loving God and our
neighbour. Therefore in this life we wish
to have no temporal possessions.

POOR IN SPIRIT

I recommend these three words to you,
namely, holy *simplicity*, *prayer*
and the *love of poverty*.
Not just poverty itself …
but love and zeal for it.

GOOD WORKS

Whatever is good pertains to God alone,
to whom belongs every good.

GOOD WORKS

Always be intent on good works,
for it is written:
'Always do something good
so that the devil will find you occupied.'

GOOD WORKS

'Idleness is the enemy of the soul',
therefore, the servants of God
must always give themselves totally
to prayer or to some good work.

GOOD WORKS

Those are given life
by the spirit of sacred scripture
who ... by word and example,
return everything to the most high
Lord God to whom every good belongs.

BLESSINGS

May God, the King of all,
bless you in heaven and upon earth.
May the Lord be mindful of your work
and of your labour,
and may a share be reserved for you
in the reward of the just.
May you find every blessing you desire,
and may whatever you ask worthily
be granted to you.

Blessings

May the Lord bless you and keep you.
May he show his face to you
and be merciful to you.
May he turn his countenance to you
and give you peace.

FORGIVENESS

I forgive my brothers,
both present and absent,
all their offences and faults,
and, in as far as I am able,
I absolve them.

FORGIVENESS

Blessed the man who is as patient
with his neighbour's short-comings
as he would wish him to be
if he were in a similar position himself.

FORGIVENESS

That person truly loves his enemy
who is not upset at any injury
which is done to himself,
but out of love of God
is disturbed at the sin
of the other's soul.

TROUBLES

Difficult struggles
are hardly ever put in the way of anyone
except where virtue has been perfected.

TROUBLES

Brief is the world's treasure,
but the punishment that follows it
lasts forever.
Small is the suffering of this life,
but the glory of the next life is infinite.

TROUBLES

They are truly peacemakers
who are able to preserve
their peace of mind
for love of
our Lord Jesus Christ,
despite all they suffer in this life.

TROUBLES

Those weighed down by sickness,
and others wearied because of them,
all of you: bear it in peace.
For you will sell this fatigue
at a very high price
and each one will be crowned
in heaven with the Virgin Mary.

SINNERS

That person sins who wishes
to receive more from his neighbour
than what he is willing to give of himself
to the Lord God.

MINISTRY

Should any of the leaders command
any of the brothers
to do something contrary to our life
or against his conscience,
he is not bound to obey,
since that is not obedience
in which a fault or sin is committed.

MINISTRY

In the name of the Lord
I ask all the brothers to learn
the tenor and sense of these things
which have been written in this life
for the salvation of our souls,
and to call them frequently to mind.

MINISTRY

Look at your dignity you brothers
[who are] priests,
and be holy since he is holy …
hold back nothing of yourselves
for yourselves,
so that he who gives himself totally to you
may receive you totally.

MINISTRY

He has sent you into the entire world
for this reason:
that in word and deed
you may give witness to his voice
and bring everyone to know
that there is no one who is all-powerful
except him.

THE HOLY SPIRIT

With God there is no respect of persons,
and the minister general of the order,
the Holy Spirit,
rests equally upon the poor
and the simple.

THE HOLY SPIRIT

You must desire above all things
to have the Spirit of the Lord
and his holy manner of working.

JUDGING OTHERS

Those who have received
the power to judge others
should exercise judgment with mercy
as they themselves desire to receive mercy
from the Lord.

HUMILITY

What you are before God
that you are and no more.

HUMILITY

When you go about the world,
do not quarrel or fight with words,
or judge others;
rather, be meek, peaceful and unassuming,
gentle and humble,
speaking courteously to everyone,
as is becoming.

HUMILITY

We must be simple, humble, and pure.

LEADERSHIP

In a rash superior
what is the power to command
but a sword in the hand of a madman?

LEADERSHIP

I would like to describe one
who would be capable
of being the leader of any army
and the shepherd of a large flock:

LEADERSHIP

One who has no private loves;
One to whom zeal for prayer
is a close friend;
One in whom the care
of the lowly and the simple
is no less pronounced
than care for the wise and the great.

LEADERSHIP

One who,
though it be their gift to excel in learning,
bears the image of pious simplicity
in actions and fosters virtue;
One who should show
an example for imitation to the rest;
One who consoles the afflicted.

LEADERSHIP

Above all else it pertains to him or her
to examine the secrets of consciences,
to bring out the truth from hidden places,
but not to listen to the talkative.

LEADERSHIP

Finally, he or she must be one
who in no way will bring down
the strong fabric of justice
by eagerness for retaining honours.

WISDOM

The worth of knowledge is proportionate
to the actions it produces;
there is no better sermon
than the practice of the virtues.

WISDOM

Give thanks to Our Lord Jesus Christ who has deigned to reveal the treasures of divine wisdom through the mouths of simple ones. For God is he who opens the mouths of infants and the dumb, and when he wishes, he makes the tongues of the simple speak very wisely.

WISDOM

Know well that in the sight of God there are certain matters which are very lofty and sublime which are sometimes considered worthless and inferior by people, while there are other things, cherished and esteemed by people, which are considered worthless and inferior by God.

WISDOM

The Lord told me that he wished me
to be a new kind of simpleton
in this world,
and he does not wish us to live
by any other wisdom than this.

PERFECT JOY

If you give sight to the blind, heal the paralysed, drive out devils, give hearing back to the deaf, make the lame walk, and restore speech to the dumb, and what is still more, bring back to life a man who has been dead four days — perfect joy is not in that.

PERFECT JOY

If you knew all languages and all sciences
and scripture, if you knew how to
prophesy and to reveal the future, the
secrets of the consciences and minds of
others — perfect joy is not in that.

PERFECT JOY

If you could speak with the voice of an
angel, and knew the courses of the stars
and the powers of herbs, knew all about
the treasures in the earth, and the qualities
of birds and fishes, animals, humans,
roots, trees, rocks and the deep waters
— perfect joy is not in that.

PERFECT JOY

If you could preach so well that you should convert all unbelievers to the faith of Christ — perfect joy is not there.

PERFECT JOY

Above all the graces and gifts
of the Holy Spirit
is that of conquering oneself
and willingly enduring sufferings, insults,
humiliations and hardships
for the love of Christ …

PERFECT JOY

if we endure cruel rebuffs patiently,
without being troubled
and without complaining,
and if we reflect humbly and charitably
[when others] speak against us
— perfect joy is there!

CHARITY AND DISCERNMENT

Where there is poverty with joy,
there is neither covetousness nor avarice.

Where there is inner peace
and meditation,
there is neither anxiousness
nor dissipation.

CHARITY AND DISCERNMENT

Where there is charity and wisdom
there is neither fear nor ignorance.

Where there is patience and humility,
there is neither anger nor disturbance.

CHARITY AND DISCERNMENT

Where there is mercy and discernment,
there is neither excess
nor hardness of heart.

CHARITY AND DISCERNMENT

Where there is fear of the Lord
to guard the house
there the enemy cannot gain entry.

The Canticle of Brother Sun

Most high, all-powerful, all good Lord!
All praise is yours, all glory,
all honour and all blessing.

To you alone, Most High, do they belong.
No mortal lips are worthy
to pronounce your name.

THE CANTICLE OF BROTHER SUN

All praise be yours, my Lord
through all that you have made,
and first my lord Brother Sun
who brings the day;
and light you give us through him.
How beautiful he is,
how radiant in all his splendour!
Of you, Most High, he bears the likeness.

THE CANTICLE OF BROTHER SUN

All praise be yours, my Lord,
through Sister Moon and Stars;
in the heavens you have made them,
bright and precious and fair.
All praise be yours, my Lord,
through Brothers Wind and Air,
both fair and stormy,
all the weather's moods,
by which you cherish all that you have made.

THE CANTICLE OF BROTHER SUN

All praise be yours, my Lord,
through Sister Water,
so useful, lowly, precious and pure.
All praise be yours, my Lord,
through Brother Fire,
through whom you brighten up the night.
How beautiful he is, how gay,
full of power and strength.

THE CANTICLE OF BROTHER SUN

All praise be yours, my Lord,
through Sister Earth, our mother,
who feeds us in her majesty,
and produces various fruits
with coloured flowers and herbs.

THE CANTICLE OF BROTHER SUN

All praise be yours, my Lord,
through those who grant pardon
for love of you;
through those who endure sickness
and trial.
Happy those who endure in peace;
by you, Most High, they will be crowned.

THE CANTICLE OF BROTHER SUN

All praise be yours, my Lord,
through Sister Death,
from whose embrace
no mortal can escape.
Woe to those who die in mortal sin!
Happy those she finds doing your will!
The second death can do no harm
to them.

The Canticle of Brother Sun

Praise and bless my Lord,
and give him thanks,
and serve him with great humility.

PRAYER

When you pray, say the Our Father, and
'We adore you, O Christ,
in all your churches in the whole world
and we thank you,
because by your holy cross
you redeemed the world.'

A Meditation on the Our Father

Our Father:
most holy, our Creator and Redeemer,
our Saviour and our Comforter.

A Meditation on the Our Father

Who art in heaven:
in the angels and the saints. You give them
light so that they may have knowledge,
because you, Lord, are light. You inflame
them so that they may have love,
because you, Lord, are love.

A Meditation on the Our Father

You live continually in them and you fill them so that they may be happy, because you, Lord, are the supreme good, the eternal good, and it is from you all good comes, and without you there is no good.

A Meditation on the Our Father

Hallowed be thy name:
may our knowledge of you become ever
clearer, so that we may realise the extent
of your benefits, the steadfastness of your
promises, the sublimity of your majesty
and the depth of your judgments.

A Meditation on the Our Father

Thy kingdom come:
so that you may reign in us by your grace
and bring us to your kingdom, where we
shall see you clearly, love you perfectly,
be happy in your company
and enjoy you for ever.

A Meditation on the Our Father

Thy will be done on earth as it is in heaven:
that we may love you with our whole heart
by always thinking of you; with our whole
mind by directing our whole intention
towards you and seeking your glory in
everything; and with all our strength by
spending all our energies and affections
of soul and body
in the service of your love alone.

A Meditation on the Our Father

And may we love our neighbours as
ourselves, encouraging all to love you as
best we can, rejoicing at the good fortune
of others, just as if it were our own,
and sympathising with their misfortunes,
while giving offence to no one.

A Meditation on the Our Father

Give us this day our daily bread:
your own beloved Son, our Lord Jesus
Christ, to remind us of the love he
showed for us and to help us understand
and appreciate it and everything that he
did or said or suffered.

A Meditation on the Our Father

And forgive us our trespasses:
in your infinite mercy, and by the power
of the passion of your Son, our Lord
Jesus Christ, together with the merits and
the intercession of the Blessed Virgin
Mary and all your saints.

A Meditation on the Our Father

As we forgive those who trespass against us:
and if we do not forgive perfectly, Lord,
make us forgive perfectly, so that we may
really love our enemies for love of you,
and pray fervently to you for them,
returning no one evil for evil, anxious
only to serve everybody in you.

A Meditation on the Our Father

And lead us not into temptation:
hidden or obvious, sudden or unforeseen.

But deliver us from evil:
present, past, or future.

Amen.

What kind of man was Francis?

WHAT KIND OF MAN WAS FRANCIS?

He kept unfailingly to his death
the resolution that he would never
turn away a poor man who asked
an alm for the love of God.

WHAT KIND OF MAN WAS FRANCIS?

He looked upon the greatest multitude of people as one person and he preached to one as he would to a multitude.

What kind of man was Francis?

Compassion for the crucified
was rooted in his holy soul.

WHAT KIND OF MAN WAS FRANCIS?

Once Saint Francis spent a whole night
in prayer saying nothing but,
'O most holy Lord, I long to love you.
O most sweet Lord, I long to love you.'

WHAT KIND OF MAN WAS FRANCIS?

Even as a young man,
Francis' spirit was
one of gentle kindness
and generous compassion
for the poor.

WHAT KIND OF MAN WAS FRANCIS?

The joy of Francis
was not in having nothing.
It was in having nothing but God.

What kind of man was Francis?

He saw God in everything,
and loved and praised him in all creation.
By God's generosity and goodness,
he possessed God in everything,
and everything in God.

What kind of man was Francis?

The realisation that everything
comes from the same source
made him call all created things
– no matter how insignificant –
his brothers and sisters,
because they had the same origin as he.

WHAT KIND OF MAN WAS FRANCIS?

The Spirit of the Lord
always points toward the other,
and thus the Spirit-filled person
is the true servant.
Therein is the poverty and humility
of Saint Francis of Assisi.

GW00838812

Guide to Life

RUNNING PRESS
PHILADELPHIA · LONDON

9 8 7 6 5 4 3 2 1

Digit on the right indicates the number of this printing

Library of Congress Control Number: 2011922838

ISBN 978-0-7624-4326-0

Running Press Book Publishers
A Member of the Perseus Books Group
2300 Chestnut Street
Philadelphia, PA 19103-4371

Visit us on the Web!
www.runningpress.com

NBCUniversal
Television Consumer Products

Contents

Introduction

Arguably one of the greatest TV shows for teens of all time, *Saved By the Bell* was one of the highest rated shows in the early '90s. The popular sitcom often touched on serious issues that real high school students face and the trials and tribulations of growing up, but also offered plenty of silly antics and adventures, and of course, laughs! This Miniature Edition™ hopes to recapture some of that laughter and fun.

With this humorous and thoughtful Guide to Life, you'll gain insightful wisdom from the words of cool trouble-maker Zack Morris, class babe Kelly Kapowski, fashionista Lisa Turtle, heartthrob jock A.C. Slater, brainiac Jessie Spano, lovable nerd Samuel

"Screech" Powers, and don't forget everyone's favorite principal, Mr. Belding.

Whether you want to take a trip down memory lane with the crew, laugh at Screech and Lisa's quibbles, or relive the Zack-Slater-Kelly love triangle all over again, these memorable characters are back to help you learn a little something about living young and carefree. Welcome to Bayside!

WORK AND PLAY

Zach: We're the perfect team.

She works hard, I hardly work!

Third place,
wow!
I once finished
fifth in an
ALF look-a-like
contest.

Zack: You look great!

Kelly: Thanks, Zack. I wore your favorite dress.

Screech: No offense, I think the dress looks better on her, Zack.

Mr. Belding: Screech, you can't elope.

Screech: Who're you calling a cantaloupe, you melon head?

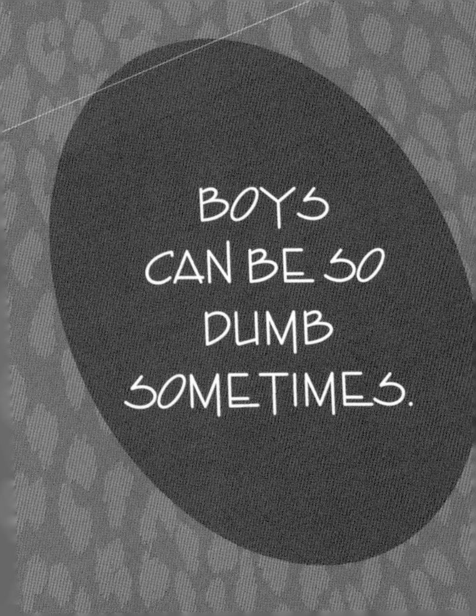

BOYS
CAN BE SO
DUMB
SOMETIMES.

Lisa: Well, Screech, maybe you're pregnant.

Screech: Oh, don't be ridiculous, Lisa. I'm not even married!

Lisa; Lisa no en casa.

Screech: I love it when you speak German!

Mr. Belding: Our history teacher is Kelly Kapowski.

Kelly: Gosh, I'm so excited!

Screech: Yeah, me too. I finally have underwear that fits!

Lisa: Screech, stop and smell the roses.

SCHOOL

RULES

Hey, hey, hey, *what* is going on here?

I LIKE SCHOOL . . .
IT'S A GOOD
WAY TO KILL TIME
BETWEEN
WEEKENDS.

Mr. Belding: Zack,
just because you always
park your car in that
same spot does not mean
it's official.

Zack: Then make it official, just like my seat in detention.

It's Saturday morning and we are in school, depressing isn't it? We are here to take this test called the SAT while I'd rather be at the beach working on my T-A-N.

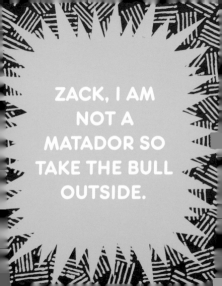

ZACK, I AM
NOT A
MATADOR SO
TAKE THE BULL
OUTSIDE.

The three worst things that can happen to a kid are measles, mumps, and midterms.

Jessie: We were discussing the obvious benefits of a female president. She's long overdue.

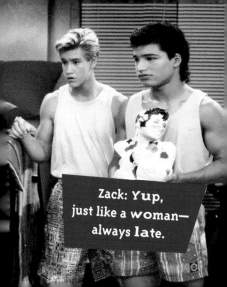

Zack: Yup,
just like a woman—
always late.

Slater: Guys are great at math. It's just a shame you weren't born a man.

Jessie: Yeah, it's a shame you weren't born one either.

Zack:
I made
gingerbread
women.

Slater:
Gingerbread
chicks.
I like it.

Jessie: For you, they should've made gingerbread pigs.

Jessie: Lisa,
you were great in the
100-yard dash.

Lisa: Oh, thanks,
but I owe my victory
to Screech.

Screech: You do?

Lisa: Oh yes, I pretended you were chasing me.

Kelly: Why aren't you at the prom?

Zack: Oh, is that tonight? Gosh, I must have forgotten.

Kelly: There must have been 100 girls who would love to go with you.

Zack: Actually 106.

Screech: Lisa, guess what I'm wearing?

Lisa: Is that mistletoe?

Screech: Yeah.
Do you want to do anything?

Lisa: Yes.
Run away.

Jessie: Slater, haven't you heard of the Women's Movement?

Slater: Sure. Put on something cute and MOVE it into the kitchen.

Screech: Will you
go to the
prom with me?

Lisa: Yeah, I'll go.

Screech: You will?!

Lisa: I'll go with
you when worms
have ears!

DATING
101

**The name
is Bond.
Screech Bond.
I have
a license
to love.**

Zack: Look, I know it's supposed to be over between us, and I know we're friends now, but Kelly, I don't feel that way. You're the only girl for me and you always will be.

Zack: Come on,
I'll walk you to class.
What've we got?

Kelly: Chemistry.

Zack: We sure do.

Kelly: Lisa, you
should give Screech
a chance.

Lisa: I'd rather give
chicken pox a
chance.

Kelly: Do you think we could get started up again?

Zack: Well, actually I'm already started up, halfway out the driveway and burning rubber.

Slater: Hi, I'm, uh, Zack's older, cooler, more happening friend, A.C. Slater.

Sandy: Ooh, what's the A.C. stand for?

Slater: Absolutely Charming.

Zack: What do you want to be when you grow up, Kelly?

Kelly: I'm thinking of becoming an actress.

Zack: Hey, you star in my dreams every night.

Kelly: Guys, this is hard. It's like choosing between two great pieces of chocolate.

Zack: Sorry, Kelly.
From now on,
you can only get zits
from one of us.

BOYS WILL
BE BOYS

Jessie: All right, concentrate, Slater, CONCENTRATE!

Slater: How can I concentrate? I'm starving! I only had four Twinkies and a box of Ding-Dongs for breakfast!

I could charge
lonely girls
to watch me flex
my muscles.

Slater: So we can't have a party—we can still have fun. We'll do, you know, guy stuff.

Screech: Yeah, it'll be great! We'll rip phone books in two and burp as loud as we want!

Hey, I don't need this pressure. I'm the captain of the wrestling team and the football team. I've got great dimples, good teeth, and the biggest muscles in school. C'mon, isn't that enough for my friends?

OINK OINK,
BABY.

I can't stand by
that backdrop.

It clashes with
my outfit!

SO MANY BOYS,
SO LITTLE
TIME.

Why not go to the boys' room and flush yourself to China?

If any one of you
sweeties dares bid
on my Slater,
I'm gonna hunt you
down in the streets
like a rabid dog.

Lisa: Girl, if I was Leslie, I would've slapped you till my hand hurt. Then I would've slapped you for making it hurt.

Screech: You know, I kissed Lisa for the first time on a bridge.

Zack: When was that?

Lisa: Right before I threw him off.

HERE'S
SOMETHING
I LEARNED IN
FRENCH CLASS:
AU REVOIR,
CREEP!

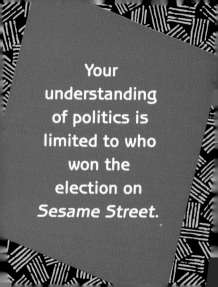

Your understanding of politics is limited to who won the election on *Sesame Street.*

THE BEST
OF FRIENDS

Screech: Zack, something terrible has just happened.

Zack: You found out Alf was a puppet?

Screech: He is?!

Zack: Jessie, don't be ridiculous, there are a lot of guys who are taller than you.

Jessie: Oh really? Name one.

Zack: Kareem Abdul-Jabbar?

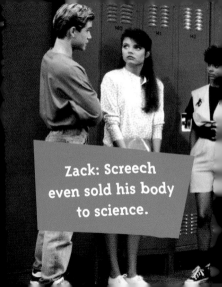

Screech: Hey, ya know what, Slater? With this microscope, your nose hairs look like the Amazon Rain Forest.

Zack: What are you
trying to say,
Screech? You want
to be a bride?

Screech: No, of
course not. But it
would be
nice to be asked.

I'M
SCREECH.
ZACK'S
GEEKY
SIDEKICK.

Zack: Allow me to recommend Zack Morris. He's cute, warm, and affectionate.

Slater: So's a cocker spaniel.

Lisa: Screech,
would you like to rejoin
the human race?

Screech: You always said
I wasn't a member.

Lisa: I'll sneak you in.

Zack: Lisa, you are looking lovelier than ever today.

Lisa: Can the sweet talk, Zack. You're giving me a zit.

Lisa: I made these friendship bracelets in Fashion Club.

Screech: Did you make one for me?

Lisa: For you, I'm making a friendship muzzle.

Screech: I'm speechless.
Lisa: That's the idea.

WORDS TO GROW ON

Zack: I'm sorry you were stuck in the file cabinet for so long.

Screech: That's okay. Just paint me blue and call me a Smurf.

You know, I've finally found out the best thing about high school. Once you graduate, you don't have to come back.

My knees were
knocking so hard
I almost
answered them!

ZACK, I'M
NOT
A STRAW.
DON'T
SUCK UP!

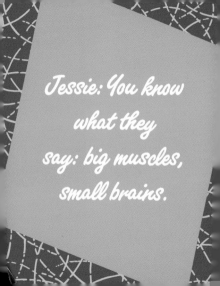

Screech:
YOU almost died . . .
you didn't have
to walk around with a
dozen eggs in your
pantyhose.

Mr. Belding:
Young lady, the men's
room is one of the
few doors that
education should NOT
open for you!

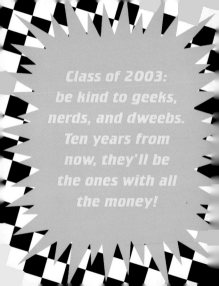

Class of 2003:
be kind to geeks,
nerds, and dweebs.
Ten years from
now, they'll be
the ones with all
the money!